Table of Contents

LIBERATION

Awakening 2008..............................

Me @ 37 2008................................

How many?? 2008...7

Liberated woman 2007.......................................8

Heart song 2007..9

38 strong (me @ 38) 2008..............................10

Alone, part 2 2009..11

MEN-TAL FREEDOM

To my baby daddy 2003....................................13

My Jamaican guy 2007.....................................14

Outside my race 2008.....................................15

Ego trippin', kickin' & slappin' 2008...................16

Is He? 2008..18

Mirror 2007..19

Bowl of soup 2008..20

Adjectives of you 2007...................................21

Wish list 2008...22

My last message 2008.....................................23

IN MY SPIRIT

Help me understand 2005..................................25

One day at a time 2007...................................26

Just thinking 2006.......................................27

Vanity chic 2008...28

She's a daddy's girl, rejected 2008......................29

"That child been here before" 2008..................31

The magnolia tree 2009............32

Nature moment 2009..............33

Prayer: Faith 2007..................34

Prayer: Discouraged 2007.........35

Relationships need real love 2008....36

Parade wave 2009...................38

CIVIL REVOLUTIONARY RIGHTS

Out to prophet, not profit 2007............40

"M" stands for Murder 2007..............41

Multi-Colored Browns© 2006.............43

Conscious journey.........................45

TRIBUTES

To my son, Jamari (Mother to son-Langston Hughes)2008......47

Cheff 2009……………………………………………….....49

SHORT STORIES

The day I **'heard'** I had HIV 2007....................51

One day in the Garden of Eden-short story 2010…...53

He's not into you-short story 2011....................61

Superfysical A-dicktion 2010.........................75

BONUS Stories & Poem:

Angel'O {short story} 82

Living room intimacy {short story} 86

New face value {poem with pic} 88

Revised: April 22, 2022

I want to take this opportunity to thank friends and family members who sincerely support me, my thoughts and style, knowing this is my gift from God to share with 'this' world.

To my cousin Sean Branch, thank you for taking the vision (cover picture) I sent to you; manifesting the version on the cover of this book into an illustration I will cherish, and many others that read this book will realize why the cover is so significant. (Love you cousin).

Mr. Andy Greene, thank you. Your brilliance of angles and poses with a camera, natural talent for capturing all my good sides assisted with the concept of this book, to make it more relevant within the pages & chapters.

I also must thank the men & women who've introduced themselves to me through seasons of their lives: good, bad, or ugly; I appreciate you.

This is my second 'Poetry' book of thoughts, beliefs, views, pain & pleasure.

ENJOY!

Thank you for your continued support.

Sincerely,

JaNyce 'NeeCee' Whiteside

LIBERATION
~~Ohio Players~~

I want to be free…

To run & play

I want to be free…

To run away

I want to be free…

To speak my mind

ALL THE TIME

AWAKENING

The stretch in the morning/ to get my limbs going/ get my thoughts flowing/ Thank you Creator/ is the first thought of the day…I am awake now. walk to the bathroom to wash dust from my face/ the taste in my mouth/ pray for a productive day/ send someone in need my way…I am awake now.

I turn on HIS light/ to bring my son out of sleep/ sit on his bed, tickle him til' he sees its me/ he is awake now & happy/ I pray he continues to live this way/ I pray he has a safe, productive day/ and learn positives lessons/ we both are awake now.

The walk to the kitchen to make coffee/ take the pill that keeps me still/because my thyroid, I'm considered ill/ I make breakfast for us both/ though mine will be cold when I get to work/ I heat it up and thank God for sustenance he provides…I am awake now.

AWAKENING

The stretch in my life/ to get my mind right/get my limbs going/keep my thoughts flowing, positively/ Thank you is the first thought of the day…. I am awake now

The walk to the bathroom to wash dust from my past/ the taste in my mouth/ I pray for positive days/ send someone to guide my way…. I am awake now

The prophet Jesus turned on the light to bring me out of sleep/ now I teach my son, positivity/ so he may understand virtue in me/ I pray for ways I want to see him blessed/ turn anger to thanksgiving and love for longer days/ God keep him in your bosom, I pray…. Keep him awake now.

My walk/ to be fed daily/ taking the pill that keeps me still/ without it I will be ill/ I struggle with fleshly members, January to December/ but I remember/ when they were in control and wow…. I'm awake and aware now.

Though my food gets cold/ dealing with the ways of this world/ I hope my work will rain on those/ be the 'manna' that will feed their soul/ I'm not expecting to take a bow/ praying for more people to awake now.

Me @ 37

Here it is, another year and yes, I'm open to the possibility life needs to be dealt with spiritually.

Changed my perception of what life should be. **Awakened** the God in me; created in HIS image, so removing the veil of fear; ascension is clear, breaking free from the boredom of physicality. I want to feel lighter, excel to the real me.

Light like—not covered with the skin of sin, but the buoyancy of the universe. To burst into a flame, heading toward Jupiter, enjoying new life in my future. This 3-dimensional reality is for the ones who don't get a ticket for the astral ride to the infinite because they hold on to **earthly** treasures.

Me @ 37, ain't crazy, some will read this and know, they are on the same level. They have learned to love, and let go of **things**, the truth of it is you already have all you need. Manifest and see what it brings.

Me @ 37 took the challenge, anyone in my path needing a hand, yes indeed I'll supply all I can. Look how good I'm doing. I speak life into my spirit every day, with a simple thank you Creator for another way, another testimony I share and dare anyone to confront their fear of love—because it's true; the world needs more of, and I vow to contribute.

Sacrifice my life, pay the price, absorb the world and caress it. My life is of the spirit, the spirit is of God and God is love, so why not live in it.

Me @ 37 is happier, healthier, excited for each breath of life; yearning to be the best wife, already a good momma, laugh at the drama trying to invade my heart & mind. I rebuke the blind, pray and let it fly HIS way and in the morning, rise in my joy. Others wonder why misery hangs around. You're comfortable in it, that's why you're bound.

Me @ 37 keeps my heart toward heaven, mind in the spirit, love never ending for anyone in need. Now I stand and wait to be richly blessed for 38.

HOW MANY TIMES???

How many times have you looked at the sky & saw a familiar shape a cloud makes?

How many times have you sat still long enough to feel the true sensation of a breeze?

How many times have the blind?

How many have you been in a store & paid attention to people you'd normally ignore?

How many times have you looked up at night & actually saw the big dipper, or listened to a conversation of birds?

How many times have the blind?

How much of nature have you heard? How many times have the blind?

How many times have you greeted someone with a phony smile?

How many times have you said, 'thank you' & meant it, for a compliment you knew you'd get?

How much attention do you pay to yourself? How much of nature have you heard? How many times have the blind?

How much time do you spend in the mirror, getting the perfect face, shape & figure? The promise of waking up tomorrow safe is slim to none. How many seconds does it take to put a condom on, or load a gun; between time of birth & death—from spirit to flesh; from spirit to flesh again?

pay to yourself? How much of nature have you heard?

How many times have the blind?

See, if you can.

Liberated Woman

Wow! As I look back on my life/ wondering how different it could have been; I'm a liberated woman, idiosyncratic in personality.

Progressively I seek maturity while letting go of mediocrity. Liberating the 2nd half of my life, reaching the bottom of the hill to 40.

Wow! As I look on my life/ I see the other kind of woman I could've become; I'm a liberated woman, free thinking.

Open mind to change, constantly I rearrange. Letting go of judgmental attributes, changing negative to positive, so when I get to the hill/mountain, I won't have to go over it, I can move it.

Wow! As I look on my life/ thankful I answer for my mistakes.

Since a child, I've been liberated. A campaigner for rights, a militant source for advice, a protester of injustice, an advocate of the black female, and sponsor of a heart, broken repeatedly.

Wow! As I look back on my life/ I have no choice but continue to liberate the second half of it.

Modernization, activist, unconventional, eccentric original.

Wow! As I look forward to the other half of my life/ I see the person I'm becoming spiritual, patient, unbiased, flexible, accessible. These words say liberal to me; words must become truth; truth must become life.

Wow! The excitement liberation can bring; shedding old lies that clog your thought pattern. Letting go of teachings you felt really mattered. Life, mentally clutter free…Liberated, logically loving me.

Heart Song

La, La, La, La. Heart song.

Bum, bum, bum, bum, bum. Heart song

My heart beats: my heart beats to the rhythm of life becoming suspended in air. Bullshit has become aware of my intelligence to it, I don't care who is offended anymore.

La, la, la, la. Heart song.

My heart beats: my heart beats to the rhythm of a new tune, developed by a higher frequency beyond the moon, planets & stars of the universe. I opened my purse & found out it didn't need a designer's name to serve the same purpose.

Letting go of labels; even the one I gave myself. God likes natural talent. I'd rather be a galaxy floater, than a Hollywood blow up. Do you know your gift? May not be like mine. Do you have a job that pays your bills? Or are you currently looking for a new career?

My heart song sings to the anthem of thankful. I'm finding my way through the haze of a world that keep's its occupants in a daze, a twirl of a wand, creating a magical outcome—because that's where most of your logic comes from.

La, La, La, La. Heart song.

Bum, Bum, Bum, Bum, Bum. Heart song.

38 Strong (me @ 38)

No one is out to hurt me.

I remind myself constantly.

You are lovable & need to act like it.

Exercising, eating better, re-evaluating my life.

Goals & dreams need to **spring** forth, before I **fall** back in the same old traps.

Your God is alive, & in time will appear in the flesh to save you from destroying yourself.

Becoming abstinent; not celibate: husbands take time to find, but an occasional bump & grind never hurt any-body.

I broke the mold of marriage after marriage. Curses have a way of making suffer for not 'falling' in place. I need to feel love from a man.

Thirty something years of learning from other PEOPLE, eight years of learning myself. Two years at the edge of forty; milestone to me. Symbolizing time before arrival: arrival of love & new life; finding shelter in God, a relationship like no other.

ALONE part 2

As I sit on the floor, in front of my closet door: crying, asking God for forgiveness- "holy spirit speak to me."

Finding myself praying more amidst the days toil. Searching again for that quiet place where I beg for— more—forgiveness; asking for yet more mercy & grace, because of people.

I must still hate myself, missing so much time in life chasing people, putting faith in learning how to be a secretarial robot, not activating the precious gift you gave me.

I got hints but kept misinterpreting the message. Virtue, I seek now; a home to share rooms with my child/ren, a husband like Proverbs 31; he will love me and understand me beyond my faults and thoughts—but maybe I was Mary Magdalene in a former body, settling for what my flesh wanted.

I'm crying now, truly writing this in prayer. I smile because I felt my heart contract.

This is Alone part 2, praying continually.

MEN~TAL FREEDOM

To my baby daddy

<u>I loved you</u>: despite how you constantly use negative energy because you have no control over me, plus I don't ask you for anything. Most men would love to have a baby momma like me.

<u>I loved you</u>: that's why I don't bother you and your soon to be wife. I'm ecstatic you have a new life.

<u>Unconditionally</u>: I love all the bitches you call me; all the hatred you & your family speak in my son's ear about me, year after year. I pray you & your family learn humility, instead of vanity for the materialistic life that possesses you. I pray that your family is safe, that's why when you call me with evil in mouth, instead of losing my couth; I rebuke you.

<u>I still love you:</u> and I'm glad you think I'm beneath you. The expensive clothes & toys you buy are the reason; why? I apologize, your love comes from a box or bag; my love comes from the daily relationship I have. I don't compare the price of a garment or a pair of shoes; money is your God, not mine—man, please work on your issues.

<u>I love you baby daddy</u>: I don't hate boo boo, I already pray for & forgave you. No matter how you and your family perceive me, my universal circumference is larger than your pockets could ever be. I apologize, I don't need money or your love to bring me fulfillment, I enjoy the peace I have without negative involvement.

Money & riches is your addiction, eternal life & internal love is worth more than a paper chasing mission. So, keep your valuables, but know their all fallible. Love will continue to hold true & no matter how much you show hate, God's love will shine, & blessings happen every time.

MY JAMAICAN GUY

I used to be spellbound by you.

You may have known it.

Wanted to love you in every way, but only got one way to show it.

Unfortunately, I wish that wasn't the only reason; how I wish there was a change in season: 'cause the feelings I have at this moment, I wanted you forever.

Enjoy our conversations when we do. I know how affectionate you can be too. You always smelled fresh with your sex appeal-and-yes; Lord, please forgive this-sex with you left me speechless (literally).

After months of sex-capades, I finally beheld our reality. I was in heavy like with you, but you just want sex with me.

Now you understand why I don't come by-or why I just call to say hi.

I can no longer be the source of gratification; next time I won't be so brazen with my consultation.

I was on a hunt when we met: be careful what you search for, may not be pleased very long with the package you get; it's only a temporary fix.

Outside my race?

I used to feel dating outside my race was taboo

There is such a shortage of dedicated black men, what is a straight black woman to do?

Between the ones in jail, younger ones dying in violence; gay downlow or ones with the virus.

What will we as black women have to face, but subsequently dating outside our race?

Ego-trippin', kickin & slappin'

He came home today in a happier mood; I'm still nursing the wounds he gave me last night

Nothing in his life has ever been right.

I will tip-toe around him, because I know his temper is quick.

He greets me in a playful manner—maybe he's feeling good today

He must've had a stress-free morning and afternoon; I wonder what he's in the mood to do.

I will tip-toe around him, because I know his temper is quick.

Dinner is ready the house is clean.

I'm tired from work, but I ask: "Are you hungry?"

He looks in the pots & pans smiling: "good job baby."

While he washes his hands, I fix his plate.

I will tip-toe around him, because I know his temper is quick.

He comes from the bathroom with something in his hands,

He strikes me with it—not again

He was just so proud of me, and

He strikes again.

I will tip-toe around him, because I know his temper is quick.

He knocks the plate of food to the floor

Shoves my face in it—I can't do this anymore

But I love him, so the punches I ignore

This is what I've settled for.

I will tip-toe around him, because I know his temper is quick.

Instead of leaving him alone, I continue to get my ass kicked. My self-esteem ain't low, I ain't in denial, my girlfriends just hatin', so now I keep quiet. They try to talk to me, so I can understand, but I am, who I am, because I want this man.

So: *I will tip-toe around him, because I know his temper is quick.*

And I will, until he kills me!

Is He?

Is he for me dear God?

Is he the cage with the missing rib?

Is he the Christ in you I seek?

Is he the one that will bring the other half of US?

Is he the form for my life til we turn to dust?

Is He?

Is he for me dear God?

Is he the soul that I must mate with?

Is he the partner I will my time with?

Is he looking like me toward the heavens praying?

Not looking for a playmate, so he can keep on playing.

I battle each day this way, hoping to understand the angle of this man; does he have a negative plan?

You know what's crazy, every time I ask these questions, I get some form of confirmation.

He is.

MIRROR

I'M YOUR WOMAN, I'M YOUR MIRROR

WHAT U SEE, IS WHAT U GET...WHAT U DO I REFLECT

JUST LIKE THE CHILD THAT OBSERVES THE PARENT: I CAN EMBARR<u>ASS</u> YOUR LIFE OR GIVE U RESPECT

I AM U, WHEN YOU'RE IN FRONT OF ME & LIE

I AM U, AS U FOLD DOWN THE COLLAR OVER YOUR TIE, TO COVER UP B4 U STEP AWAY.

I AM WHAT U VIEW AS U SHAPE YOUR GOATEE, MAKING SURE EACH LINE IS STRAIGHT, NO HAIR OUT OF PLACE B4 U STEP AWAY. YOUR MIRROR SEES U EVERY DAY.

AS I REFLECT THE LIES & CHEATING: WITH ALIBIS, ARE U THINKING–ABOUT MY REFLECTION OF U ON MY SECRET RENDEZVOUS?

I GOT TIRED OF SEEING YOUR IMAGE IN THE MIRROR, SO I CHANGED MY HAIR COLOR & PUT ON A DIFFERENT SHADE OF EYE SHADOW.

NOW MY EYES ARE ATTRACTING A DIFFERENT VISION IN THE MIRROR.

U STOOD IN FRONT OF ME & I 'CRACKED' UP, BECAUSE I SAW YOUR FLAWS. FOR THE 1ST TIME, I SAW YOUR UGLINESS, YOUR AGE SPOTS; U THOUGHT YOUR MIRROR ONLY REFLECTED U.

I'M YOUR WOMAN, I'M YOUR MIRROR

WHAT U SEE, IS WHAT U GET

WHAT U HAVE DONE TO ME: I NOW REFLECT.

Bowl of Soup

When I get sick,

Chicken noodle with chunks of chicken is best.

When it's cold outside,

I curl up with a good book, some crackers & clam chowder.

When I was a child, alphabet soup was fun. I made words & ate them—Ha, Ha, Ha: get it yet?

A bowl of soup is a multi-purpose meal; according to the way you feel.

A bowl of soup can make you feel better; warm you inside when it's cold outside or make your meal fun.

Can I be your bowl of soup?

Adjectives of you

(From your secret admirer)

Tall, handsome; predictable wardrobe that doesn't matter.

Pleasant: always smiling, when you look back to speak, despite the many times you enter and exit the office door. My cheeks turn red, my heart quivers. I blush.

Are you married, or just a baby daddy? I don't see a ring; but nowadays that means nothing. Are you interested in me, or are your smiles out of courtesy?

The adjectives of you describe what I seek: quiet, simple, respectful—meek.

I've dealt with all types, now I don't 'believe the hype' I'm older, wiser and tired of chasing; running into lovers not friends, I was complacent then.

Adjectives of you are descriptions of what I want to know. I want to approach but, my mind says wait—this is a work in progress, watch for an update.

Wish list

I wish I could be the aspirin or ibuprofen you need to soothe your mental throbs of life.

You seem so stressed or frustrated when you place your hand on your head amid a conversation on the phone.

I wish I could be the other person opposite you, on the phone sometimes. I know you're conducting business; I want you in my business too.

I wish I could melt into those masculine arms of yours and feel the security of years to come and never take those arms for granted.

I wish I could be an outfit in your closet, and you wear me all day, and I would conform to every crease of your body.

I wish I could be your relaxation. Where you let go of the world and worries of life; focus, if only a moment on me, one of the things that makes you happy.

I wish I could be a vase or a piece of furniture in your home. If I just collect dust, feeling the breeze as you walk by, or get comfortable on me is where I'd rather be.

I know this is <u>my</u> wish list, and if life were to grant me this wish <u>you</u> would never wish for anything more.

My last message

Hey, you; I called you last night, remember I wanted to celebrate with you. I was feeling right,

Blessed with an increase for my daily life.

You were the first to cross my mind, wanted to chill, haven't seen your smile in a while,

Seems you're up to the same tricks. The call went straight to voicemail, that didn't make sense.

You have a business.

I finally get the message: I'm not your rib.

I stopped questioning what is wrong with me. Why I can't seem to past the beginning.

Why I'm never winning, but steadily dwindling, in advances & chances to be spending.

Time to be ending, because all I'm doing is wasting it on **wishing**

I finally get the message: my essence to you isn't worth rendering.

Resolutions for a new year, is like revelations for this woman here. Baggage from previous life & loves has no value.

I know the caliber of woman I am. I am not designed for just **any** man. I get lost in my own program, but it's the universe that has the upper hand.

I finally get the message: my God already picked the man; I need to accept the plan.

This is my last message: Thank you for crossing my path, allowing me to experience another chance to see why patience, keeps me from being disappointed again.

IN MY SPIRIT

Just bee's & things & flowers

~~Roy Ayers~~

"Everybody loves the sunshine

HELP ME UNDERSTAND!!

I'm not an atheist. I do believe in a creator of all things, at one time considered the big bang theory.

Religion is a territorial practice it seems.

I have studied, practiced, prayed, abstained, stop smoking, stop socializing, stopped eating certain foods. Stopped everything I used to do, all in the name of: Christianity, Islam, Nuwaubu, Gods & Earth's, A.M.E., 7th Day Adventist, practically every religious entity has a lil' piece of worth.

I have been Church of Christ baptized; Baptist dipped as well; so why do I still believe I'm going to hell?

Religion is just like everything else on this planet—a choice.

John 4:24__ "God is a 'spirit' and they that worship HIM, must worship Him in spirit and in truth."

One day at a time

One day at a time—I am shedding my ego and selfish ways

One day at a time—bringing better days.

One day at a time—I am thankful for my consciousness

One day at a time—getting closer to salvation, with each step.

One day at a time—Staying focused on my walk

One day at a time—laughing at my arrogance in thought, my spirit is no longer for sale: because is already bought.

One day at a time—Learning the true of spirituality and God

One day at a time—God is not religion in a building where doors are 'locked', but all around us and in our hearts. We have His 'key' just unlock.

One day at a time— 'They that worship Him, must worship Him in spirit and in truth'. Not in a confession booth.

One day at a time—Wanna' live like Yeshua; be his student, learning to walk in faith not in fear. Obediently, diligently; daily building trust and loyalty with the Lord for my future's years.

Want to be released from the beast of burden; opened my secret curtain of light and decided to fight.

The devil is a liar

The devil is a con. The devil is the master of this; his world, we live on.

One day at a time—Going blind from who I used to be. Humility, honesty, glory to Thee.

The One who daily sets my spirit free. The One who walked the earth before me.

The FIRST revolutionist for freedom, the freedom of who we are spiritually.

Just thinking....

Of days waking up, smothered in the arms of a man who unconditionally loves & adores me...

Thank GOD for mercy

Mornings sharing coffee/tea with specialty bread, in my breakfast nook with friends reminiscing about past experiences....

Thank GOD for his grace

Day & nights I will spend in the hospital with my son, over a broken bone or illness....

Thank GOD for strength

Moments I made the right decision & a blessing followed....

Thank GOD for faith

Times when my faith will be compromised, but with prayer I win the battle....

Thank GOD for wisdom/understanding

How many times I've been saved from death, without realizing it....

I thank GOD for his son, because the WORD & SACRIFICE he made, have made my days (good or bad) blessed ones.

Vanity Chic

I walk this way because I'm on a hunt, strutting my physique because I know what men want

I am shallow, & carry a designer bag of tricks

I am what? A Vanity Chic

Super model status, video vixen of sorts; Politicians, Dope boys & drawn to sports

Don't want a 9 to 5 square or simp, Fed-Ex UPS, um um: I'm all about expense, because I am what? A Vanity Chic

I can spend some money on my vanity, to be chic on your arm for the world to see. Loving you? I don't give a hoot, all I care for is spending your loot,

I'm not here for thin or thick, I am what? A Vanity Chic

I've been around just like a harlot, the difference is: I act more important,

I'll have your kids or play your wife, just so I can be set for life, the games I play are for my security & fit. I am what? A Vanity Chic

I must be 1st on the scene, make-up by MAC not Maybelline. Stay in boutiques & upscale shops, supporting my ego, letting you call the shots. I can Mrs. Submissive, even help you start a business.

I have plenty of selfishness, that's why you fall so quick. I am what? A Vanity Chic.

I can take your fame & add to it, my beauty, my body your conduit: as long as your bank account at least 7 figures rich & your pockets stay thick: I am what? A V A N I T Y C H I C.

She's a Daddy's Girl: Rejected

She ponders reasons why, after forgiving her mother; her mother does not have a better relationship with her.

Daddy's Girl: Rejected

Slipping & sliding with men in her path, so many let her down, failing at being a man.

Daddy's Girl: Rejected

The role of father & mother never hailed true in her life, so she fell for the vice of street life,

But she was still **Daddy's Girl**

Always wishing for acceptance; not approval, that had no protection & phony affection.

Is there anyone in this 'world' who knows how to love this **Daddy's Girl?**

Like the child she is, she loves like HIM, only to wind up: Rejected, Disrespected, Virtuously Disconnected & hurt, she continues to love—everyone.

Despite the rejection & pain, she sighs a lot and prays.

When she's gone, wonder if anyone would be amazed; if they remember how she cared, even when she stared at the sky & cried:

"Help me father to understand why so much selfishness upon this land, all I want is to share your love with my fellow man."

Following footsteps of her oldest brother, she patterns ways to be like no other.

That's how she's learned what's expected: She's a Daddy's Girl, in this 'WORLD' and that is why she's been **REJECTED**

Psalm 66:20—"*Praise be to God, who has not rejected my prayer or withheld his love from me!*"

"THAT CHILD BEEN HERE BEFORE"

The next time I begin life, I'm going to aim for more knowledge of you. This life has given me 'awakening' of my potential.

Understanding loving others, truly after they hurt your heart & made your soul weep. This life has brought the man I am to love: my son, even if the man to love never comes in this lifetime.

Next lifetime, I will listen more as my journey begins thru the 40 years it took to reach this wilderness.

I should've said "NO", to Satan when he promised me the world; then cheated me, after I did everything, he wanted me to.

I may lack knowledge of you, but mercy passed all my tests; grace showed me how to be virtuous (again), & favor?

Favor kept me blessed, because as I said before, 'this life has given the awakening of my potential', my eternal life has just begun.

So next life everything that has awakened me, I will have knowledge of. Next time you talk to me in the womb, I will glorify you better & love you even more.

To have you smile on me is key, for my lifetimes.

The Magnolia Tree

One day I stood under a magnolia tree, avoiding the rays of the sun.

As the wind blew, I felt the breeze & smelled the sweet nectar of the magnolia tree.

A tree often seen, but never smelled, I appreciate the aroma that overwhelmed me: briefly stood in submission at the fruition, of the magnolia tree.

Gods sweet gift to nature that blooms & consumes, anyone conscious enough to notice the gracious scent, of the Magnolia Tree.

Nature Moment

I saw a red robin & a squirrel playing in the grass,

A dragonfly whizzed by my eyes, disguised in a black & green body suit.

Nature on a Saturday morning.

I enjoy sitting on my balcony, listening & watching; taking a break from concrete streets, buildings filled with cubicles of people glued to their seats.

The birds are doing their morning chatting—the conversations are harmonious—I wonder how a bird sounds laughing.

The breeze is blowing, trees burst & bloom in all green hues. All I hear is nature, not the hum of machines.

Nature is now the moment.

PRAYER: Faith

Father, I come to you with a weary mind, quivering heart, full of pride. I need you.

Why can't I believe you for all my needs, step out on Faith every day, for your love to heed.

Don't leave me father, I'm planting my 'mustard seed'.

Why is it so hard when we fall apart; quick to call your name, we need you to save the day; then once you do, we don't even pray to say 'thank you. I'm guilty too.

I come to you father, with repentance of sins, my heart would be open, my mind just won't give in. Why do we get so bent out of shape for things we can't persuade; what we cannot get because, we can't feel it, see it, but want the benefit; my faith sporadic I know, but your mercy & favor keep me humble; I am moving, though slow,

I won't let go; or is it you that holds on to me, because you see my diligence for your resilience to be with you eternally.

You unconditionally love a nation of people elected, to take the trip to heaven.

Yes, I will be there: getting spiritually in shape, running the race with my armor & breastplate. I come to you like I'm supposed to, in my closet of quietude. Peace, be still because you have already revealed

To 'FAITHFULLY keep calling on you.

AMEN

PRAYER: Discouraged

Spirit within, please hear my moan/ although we are one, I act like I'm alone.

Asking for help with **strength** today, I'm too to weary to wrestle this flesh my way.

I'm asking for **your** mental stability to sustain my selfish mentality. I feel the anger & shortness in temper, when I get this way, please make me remember the love I have; lead me back to that path.

Spirit within I rebelled again. Give me the mind of humility, the body of tranquility, & help me keep my composure amid the enemy.

When I wake up happy & full of joy, the enemy begins plotting to destroy the vision for a positive outlook, now I know how JOB felt, that's why I meditate in your book of knowledge & promise to pray for you to intercede for my need, that is why I thank you in advance for the chance that will save my life.

Spirit within, please hear my moan, I am discouraged today, but I know I'm not alone.

Amen

Relationships need real Love

No one seems to desire relationships anymore.

A quick fix & score. One night with you and the thrill is gone, no more lifetime guarantees, lust is attentive now, love is ignored.

No one seems to value loving someone beyond their faults.

Our selfishness warrants only what we want. He may like you a lot but playing with your emotions to manipulate your thoughts. She may care for you in a certain way; it's your financial amenities that make her stay.

No one seems to realize it's not about quota, how many women you can play with, when you have a true one at home. Women have become like men as well even paying his bills, & younger men look for older women.

Someone, please guide me to the room with a view of genuine men, who desire genuine women. A woman with compassion; a woman with a gift, a woman who loves strong & uplifts.

I am as blind as 3 mice, as green as artificial grass, as sad as the face in the theatre mask.

No one seems to know STDs are happening in our thirties & forties, even the elderly; HIV has authority over the black community.

Women are not supposed to smell like the sea, men are carriers of most sexually disease: asymptomatic, meaning no feeling, no burning, no itching: BV, Chlamydia, etc.

Someone, please point me in the direction of a man with affection, spirituality, honor & family mentality. A man, who appreciates the woman he has, knows the meaning of everlasting life & love.

Thinks monogamy ain't some type of wood, or a game. Gets down on his & prays; with me, for me & our family.

No one seems to understand God's plan, everything going on in this country is the reflection of Sodom Gomorrah & Babylon. Sexual perversion, adultery, idolatry: it's getting worse, the victims are getting younger—beasts' hunger is getting worse—thirst more prevalent: control their mind—control their spirits.

No one seems to desire relationships anymore.

We all want a quick fix & score.

There will be no more everlasting lifetime guarantees, unless you get a Relationship with the Lord.

Amen

Parade Wave

Waving.

Waving in the wind.

Hearing life passing,

passing life; hearing life.

Passing, hearing.

Crying in my heart.

Soul, crying: "Help me!"

Help my heart heal,

heal my heart, Help me!

Waving.

The wind, crying as life is passing.

Hearing life waving in the wind,

passing my heart; waving.

Hearing life passing, crying in my heart: "Help Me!"

Because my people have forgotten me, they have burned incense to vanity, and they have caused them to stumble in their ways from the ancient paths; to walk in paths in a way not cast up.

Jeremiah 18:15

CIVIL REVOLUTIONARY RIGHTS!

Out to PROPHET, not PROFIT

I don't always write poetry about mushy things,

I write poetry, I hope, makes a change.

People interpret the same meanings in different words; repetition on every level will reach more when it's versed.

I don't often write poetry about material things; I appreciate the richness living in the spirit brings.

Loving yourself, & helping others understand, the gift of a 'hobby', is your enterprise—manifest it, nurture it, watch how YOU, grow inside.

Most of you don't even know your purpose. Some don't bother to enlist, for the service—too content with how you already exist.

We need less podium speakers & false preachers, & more: '<u>COMMUNITY ACTIVISTS & LEADERS.</u> Get off the stages & 'pull*pits*'

Be out to 'PROPHET, not PROFIT.

I don't write poetry to feed the ego; in a haystack, I need more needles; to join in this battle, not one yet.

I'm not to profit, but PROPHET.

"M" Stands for "M"urder

Ha, ha check this out: M= murder & coincidentally; 'M' is the letter of the alphabet with the 13th, degree. Also 'M' is a letter of choice in black American historical prophesy.

Let me explain why that's deep to me:

M is for murder & **M**edger Evers too, who died trying to uplift the integrity of me & you.

M is for murder & **M**alcom X, one of our most militant prophets.

M is for murder & Bob **M**arley, Rastafari has a message not just for I-n-I, call to mind the many genocides.

M is for murder & **M**arcus Garvey, whose dream of emancipation of a nation back to the land of their creation, was killed by the obvious need, he wanted our people free.

M is for murder & **M**artin, I know why his las name was King, do I need to remind anyone of his 'Dream?'

M is for **M**uhammad, the prophet of Islam, who was considered dumb, but the revelations he received are the Genesis to the Quran.

M is for murder & **M**ahatma (Ghandi), like Martin, (King), was for non-violence, & he too was assassinated for peace.

M is for murder & **M**andela, first name Nelson (d: 12/5/2013), after 27 years behind bars of oppression; still became president of South Africa; won a Nobel prize for peace, though he was treated like a beast.

M is for **M**oses, "LET MY PEOPLE GO!" God is still looking for '**M**' people.

M is for **m**ovement, which is what they all wanted, to keep a **m**onumental society out of darkness.

M stands for murder, all our prophets have died, but not in vain, we need to adhere to our history OUR culture, & stop committing mental suicide.

MultiColored Browns©

Multicolored Browns are the basic hues of earth.

The upright standing silhouettes casting from our environment.

We are the color of clay, beige like sand,

We are the color of roots/ bark of trees: cedar, cherry, & mahogany.

We are the color of honey & pecans, all natural brands, no artificial ingredients, made by man.

God & earth created life: out of the **darkness** came light.

I hope as you read the previous line, you understood it: God & earth created life: out of **darkness** came light, even from the caves.

I speak metaphorically sometimes, to see how many minds, I can reach, how many minds have risen from sleep? Because I'm heartbroken to see,

This beautiful earth keeps shaking to the same quaking.

We may as well resort to caves & dwell, instead of 'the Queen of Sheba', our women mimic, snow white, & ariel: bleaching skin, unnatural colored eyes & disposition.

MultiColored Browns, WAKE UP!

Create the Nation that will educate OUR youth,

Produce more fruit like, teachers, philosophers, scientists, doctors, artists & astronauts.

Communities so self-sufficient, our milk & honey will be running the country.

Am I not the only one with this vision? I want to see another black community like Eatonville in Florida, start teaching lessons like those to your sons & daughters.

Conscious Journey

Traveling in my consciousness, this cycle of life. I see the defects of the education I received from family.

I don't hide behind the veil of fuckery committed before me. The lies, secrets; the denied hatred that started it all, I'm the product of a same lineage, but aren't we all?

Traveling in my consciousness, this cycle of life. I see the defects of the education I received from teachers.

I don't give a shit about the whitewash history taught to keep them uplifted, my history is Native & African: history shows these tribes are consistently destroyed in the system of white man.

Traveling in my consciousness, this cycle of life. I see the defects of the education I received from niggas. Yes, nigga's, can't call them all men; a man respects, a man caresses, a man works a job or invests in himself the best business, (truest legal hustle). A man upholds responsibility, accountability & self-control.

A Nigga manipulates responsibility of others to get by or get him through, what about you:

Momma's boy, Napoleon complex control freak for the 'shorties', woman beater, child molester, coward with a gun- and my favorite: 'the wannabe' (you name it; he wanna be it). All the symptoms of Narcissism.

Traveling in my consciousness, this cycle of life, I see alters I've built to worship: burning them down & walking away, with diploma from the education from the school of the 'blind'.

Attending a 'Technical' school with 'honors', strategic 64-book course, 'fast' learning toward 'spiritual' growth, & when I graduate; walk across that stage to get my GED, (Gods Everyday Disciple),

I will attend 'Heavenly' college for that eternal degree.

TRIBUTES

To my son, Jamari

(Paired with poem 'Mother to Son' by Langston Hughes)

Langston wrote: 'Life for me ain't been no crystal stair'',

Me: I've been living in a concrete jungle instead.

'It's had tacks in it.'

Me: I'm a-tacked by consistent but ephemeral, pokes & pinches of a life full of dissension.

'And splinters'

Me: from heartache. People who have clotted the veins of appreciation, & ulcers of selfishness.

'And boards torn up, & places with no carpet on the floor—bare.'

Me: Bare: my soul was at times & continues to be. Naked with disgust from the trust I put in lust instead of love, feel like I shortchanged you from masculinity; please forgive me, my son.

'But all the time'

Me: God was in my bones, caressing my character, keeping me whole, keeping me safe, keeping me; OH, keeping me close.

'I'se been a-climbin' on,'

Me: Leaning toward faith & trusting in the Lord.

'And reaching landin's'

Me: expanding my love for all.

'And turning corners,'

Me: knocking out strongholds.

'And sometimes goin' in the dark'

Me: unable to focus, because of rejection & being ignored.

'Where there ain't been no light,'

Me: I still must fight & keep holding on.

'So, boy, don't you turn back,'

Me: or let this world destroy you.

'Don't you set down on the steps'

Me: of life & get comfortable or bored, keep striving for better than before.

'Cause you finds it's kinda hard,'

Me: without loyalty to yourself, education of their schools to protect yourself, against their fools.

'Don't you fall now,'

Me: keep believing in you, keep your head in the 'cloud' of HIS spirit, place faith & trust in Him & from every life battle, you will be delivered.

'For I'se still climbin,'

Me: and praying for you to be a successful black man, in a world against you.

'And life for me ain't been no crystal stair,'

Me: I'm a black woman so baby; stay aware, this life is full of struggle, contention; not to mention, pit falls & despair, for any son or daughter left alone in a world, to be mentally & emotionally slaughtered.

Cheff (for Allen James)

You silly: like a grasshopper hopping backwards.

You versatile: like a top ten designer working a polka dot, plaid ensemble.

You humble, like the spiritual meaning of this poem, you make me smile every time I look at yours.

You open doors, like the way you're being my mentor.

I needed to let you know. You alright with me, we 'buddy' like De La Soul & Monie.

Got my mental quiet for a moment, & these were my thoughts: Peace to my brother, may you sleep tight; now I need a vibe by you, to turn out my light.

SHORT STORIES

The day I <u>heard</u> I had HIV

The letter from the health department, read like this in so many words: "Your lifestyle has caught up with you, and you have been a naughty girl. 'You have contracted something possibly, we wanna' make sure it's **positive**ly **HIV**."

It didn't mention those 3 capital letters but, knowing that was the only test I took, didn't make it better.

So, I called the number to make the appointment; now, reflecting on my enjoyment and, considering I'm only 19, with plenty life and yes, I have **BIG** dreams.

Two days from now comes the answer to 'It.' Do I or do I not; is the question: I reminisce on the many times I was promiscuous, and wow; I hadn't realized how reckless I've been, not listening to the words of the wise.

The day has come; in the office I begin to pray, "Dear God, forgive me for my sins, I really didn't know what I was doing." My heart begins the beat of fear, the butterflies come out their cocoons; floating in my belly as I enter the room.

The counselor comes in with her folder and pen. I try reading her facial expression, but there is none.

"Well young lady your test is positive, according to the CDC that means you have **HIV**. 'Don't lose hope, you can live your life, just not as carefree as you may want to be."

She broke everything down and gave me pamphlets to read. My next steps were to see a doctor for more testing; try to locate the one who infected me: a task I focus on fearfully.

I found my old black book and pictures, sitting on my bed I start to cry. Here I am 19, **HIV** positive, and scared. "WHYYY!" I scream, this must be a dream; but the pinch, didn't wake, just bruised me. I'm dying from ignorance overcoming.

After two weeks of calls and threats on my head, the clinic calls-I thought-to check on my progress; to inform me the paperwork was misinterpreted, and my test is negative. She called to apologize for the mistake; I was already on knees, thanking God for His mercy and grace; plus, another chance.

I made a vow then, to be abstinent and date; having unprotected sex is a deadly game to play.

ONE DAY IN THE GARDEN OF EDEN-*created 12/19/2010 (revised 5/2018) This is a story of fiction although the event; remains 'timeless.'*

One morning in the Garden of Eden, Adam & Eve had an argument. Adam, has-no doubt-been given dominion and authority over the garden, so apparently, he was always right.

He reminded Eve of his position during the argument, reprimanding her to 'submit'. She submitted; silently walking away to cool down.

Adam was created before her, Eve also knew she wasn't created 'before' him, but from a rib of his; then 'presented' to him, with a different state of mind.

Adam's arrogance roared loudly this morning, and Eve sought peace from Adam's repetitive words.

Eve quietly spoke to herself as she walked:

"Man was created first; and I, the flesh of his flesh, but wo-man doesn't think like man. I was introduced to him. Surely, he proves I'm of no help to him with only demands. I'm not a beast, I'm his help meet."

A few more minutes of walking, Eve finds a tree close by for shade. The trunk of the tree is enveloped among short blades, of thick grass, soft enough for Eve to rest from the radiating heat of the sun.

Settling in comfort she tilts back; her eyes face a sky filled with cotton puff clouds; altering themselves in slow motion: forming different shapes against a baby blue, back drop.

Eve is in prayer, when her name is heard. It wasn't Adam's voice; the voice was coming from above her.

"Eve, Eve, why do you pray under this tree?' Why are you on this side of the garden alone?"

Eve opens her eyes in bewilderment. Here, in the midst, of the garden she sat rested beneath, the tree of good and evil. The personal conversation; finding shade, exhaling, gazing at the clouds & sky praying; she's stumbled onto forbidden grounds.

Facing the tree-not discerning the voice-Eve speaks at the trunk, "Am I disturbing your growth tree?"

The limbs and leaves above her shake, exposing a rather unique form of life.

The serpent can appear in all shapes, sizes and likeness.

The serpent *that* day, must've been appealing to Eve.

"Whoa, were did *you* come from?" Asks Eve.

"Before your time," says the serpent.

Eve's eyes inspect this creature thoroughly, "Yeah, I haven't seen anything like you; are there others like you around?"

"Why yes, there are. What I wanna know' is how did you; Queen, find yo' way under this tree? You know you're asking for trouble, right?"

"The man-& I, disagreed this morning. I walked out to clear my mind of his arrogance, and here I stand. You know you really, are a peculiar looking life form, do you bite?"

"She's vulnerable now," the serpent slithered to himself.

"No Queen, I don't bite, unless you want me to. 'Say, since you're beneath this tree; it must be for a reason, right? I mean you don't just wander off from the King who makes you submit for nothing, huh?"

The serpent waits for Eve's reaction.

"You have a point there peculiar one, if only the man's attitude wasn't so harsh or full of pride at times, he could behold the true nature of why I was brought to him."

The serpent giggled with pleasure. It's time to strike, "Queen, you know there is a way to handle that."

A burst of excitement shot through Eve, "How peculiar one. How do I help the man, appreciate me?"

Before the serpent could respond, Eve rubs her hand over her torso due to hunger. The serpent went in for the kill.

"Queen, the tree you stand under is ripe with fulfilling fruit."

"No peculiar one, the man & I are forbidden to eat from this tree, or we will die."

"Says who?" blurts the serpent.

"The one who created the man & I.' Are you allowed to eat from this tree?"

The serpent laughs, "Now Queen, would I be in this tree if I couldn't eat of it? The only reason your creator doesn't permit you & the man to eat from this tree, is because HE knows once you taste its nectar- you will be a peculiar one to him. Your eyes will be opened to a better perception of why you and the man were created."

The serpent cut a small piece of fruit with his sharp nails-"eat."

The serpent ate the rest to show Eve, nothing will happen. Eve hesitated to make sure the serpent was being honest. The serpent remained in the same form and didn't die. Eve looked at the fruit she is forbidden to touch. Nectar, dripping from the fruit between the serpent's sharp nails, inviting her to taste. She delicately retrieved it from the serpent.

Eve licked the fruit first. Rolling her tongue around her pallet for flavor didn't yield a taste. She bit; and flavors she'd never experienced danced inside her mouth.

Eve waited for something different to happen, but the trick isn't done unless Adam fell too.

Falling on her knees she asked the serpent, "what is this called?"

The serpent responds, "someday it will be called chocolate, and every wo-man born of this garden will crave it in all its forms."(especially in men)

The serpent plucked 3 more pieces of fruit, prescribing to Eve how to use it with Adam. Eve admired the intelligence of this peculiar creature.

"Honey, if you want the man to appreciate you, give him half a piece: you eat the other half and both of you will feel euphoria."

"Are you sure this fruit will change his ways?" asked Eve.

"Can an eagle fly?" said the serpent.

The serpent also admonished Eve to sneak a piece of fruit the next time the man's arrogance revolted against her, obliging the confidence to cuss his ass out and make him leave.

"Wow, peculiar one this fruit is that powerful."

"Queen, this fruit holds the power of the Gods! You just happened to be in the right place and time to receive. That's the reason you're here, you needed my counseling."

The time of day is approaching for Eve to prepare the man's lunch.

Eve took a second bite of the fruit as she walked back home. Her belly appeared full after the second bite.

With newfound freedom, she contemplates; instead of cooking, she will share the fruit with Adam and cook later. Eve meets Adam at the entrance of their abode.

"Adam, I'm not cooking lunch, but I'd like you to taste this fruit. I ate two bites, and my hunger has been quenched."

Adam was famished. Without hesitation, he bit the fruit and he too; fell on his knees, "What on earth is this?" looking up at Eve.

Suddenly, Adam and Eve started convulsing. A transformation of energy disfigured them from heavenly form to a physical form of density.

They were no longer radiant energy and light. They're heavier, stretchy and naked in this form. Adam scrambled to find material to cover them, but leaves were all they could find in the garden.

When Eve prayed under the tree, she asked the teacher to guide her. She asked the teacher to talk to Adam about his arrogance and disposition. The teacher didn't come swiftly after her prayer, but HE always shows up in the 'nick of time'.

The teacher's voice was strong and universal. His voice traveled with the wind in the coolness of the day calling Adam and Eve. The couple were hiding in the trees and would not answer.

The teachers voice called Adam again, this time Adam answered.

"I am here teacher. I heard your voice in the wind, and we are afraid."

"Afraid?" asked the teacher.

"Afraid of what, Adam?"

Adam steps out from the brush and trees with his wife, "we are naked."

The teacher asked them, "who told you that? 'Let me guess, somebody ate from the tree I asked y'all not to eat from, didn't you?"

Adam spoke first, "This woman you introduced me to, it's her fault, she tricked me into eating it. 'Talking bout' 'here taste this, cause' I'm not cooking.

The teacher looked at Eve, "so it is true!"

In her new form, Eve realized who the peculiar being was: "the serpent beguiled me, and I did eat."

Listening to the chastisement, the serpent hangs from a branch in the tree above where the teacher is standing, "I told you. These beings you created would be weak. They can't even follow instructions properly. To think you want me to bow down to them. You know you need to stop playing."

The teacher turns to the serpent, "You don't think I know what's going on? I created all of this, and you think I don't know what happened here. I planned all this.'

'OK, first things first: serpent, since you like that sneaky slithering form you're in; you will continue to sneak and slither. The snakes of the earth will be your seed and I place hatred and enmity, between your seed and the woman's seed. Your seed will strike the heels of men, and metal will chop the heads of your seed.

'Wo-man: you're still a virgin, and basically single. When the man and you have sex and you conceive, baaaaby; the pain and sorrow you feel gonna' make you think about that piece of fruit you ate. Oh, and those words the serpent told you bout' cussing the man out-NOT gonna' happen. If you don't submit to your husband, you will be raising them babies by yo'self, how bout' that.

'Now, we come to Mr. Adam: Who was dominion given to?" asked the teacher.

In a low tone Adam says: "me."

"Huh? Speak up." snaps the teacher.

"You did."

"You didn't know the woman prayed before all this happened; I breathed into the woman a different consciousness, called 'emotions'. The woman will suffer more emotionally but was to be your help meet. Arrogance and power are what causes men to treat others with disrespect and callousness. Why do you think the serpent is where he is?

'Because you have acted harshly, all power I relinquish from you. From this day on, you are banished from this Garden. You will have to teach yourselves how to build your own and feed yourselves, eating that which you find along the way and hope it doesn't kill you."

The teacher kicked all three of them out the Garden and left. Adam and Eve found a patch of land to begin new lives, the serpent went in hiding, waiting for the chance to strike again.

Adam and Eve conceived Cain, then Abel.

Strike 2: you know the serpent was ready, right?

The teacher is ready too, so he allows the earth to turn in accordance with HIS plan. The Earth is a ball of karma now; as the earth goes around, it comes around; as above, so below, and God is STILL in control.

He's not into you

created 10/2010 (revised 5/2018)

Loray and Monica have been neighbors and friends since fifth grade. Monica stands at 5'8, with shoulder length hair; dark complexion, bushy eyebrows, long eyelashes, thick hips, and a smile that captivates.

Loray, is two inches shorter than Monica; bowlegged, pecan tan, Short natural hair, big round eyes and skinny. Both young ladies are 16, and seniors in high school.

Jeremy also grew up with Loray & Monica, sharing the same street and zip code a year later.

Facing the street, Jeremy lives in the house four doors down-to the left- from Monica. Jeremy is the neighborhood pain in the ass. You know, the boy who tries to get with every girl on the block, but too freakin' annoying and tells all your business.

Growing up his hormones were worse than a cat in heat. Jeremy is a senior as well. He and Monica are the same height. Jeremy is a shade darker than beige; he dons a mo-hawk style haircut, an earring in his left ear, a crackling voice and full of pranks.

The weekends here. Monica & Loray arrive home Friday from school meeting on their front porches, for fresh evening air and conversation. Makes no sense to call each other on the phone.

Loray and Monica are discussing plans for the next week, when Loray see's Jeremy speaking with his next-door neighbor: a new addition to 13th Street; a rather handsome addition:

"Monica, don't be all obvious; but we have a handsome new brother on the block."

With a bowl of cereal in her hand, Monica casually turns to the left, "damn he fine, how we miss that?"

"OK? what you talkin' bout." says Loray.

The stare- from the two- was felt down the block; Jeremy waved and continued talking. Monica & Loray weren't prepared for a Jeremy interrogation, they needed to get cute first. After a slight alteration, with soap and water and an outfit change:

"So, Jeremy, when did our new neighbor move in?", asks Loray.

"They moved in last week; you mean you two nosy bots didn't peep that?"

"Shut up punk!" shouts Monica.

"I think he has an older brother too, so both of you can have one." Jeremy walks away, in route to the corner store.

His name is Marco; 17, height is 6'2, chiseled shoulders bulging. Almond shaped eyes, defined abs, deep voice, muscle tone legs. Yeah, this brother works out hard. His family relocated from Chicago.

"What you think Monie, should we walk past the house and scope it out?"

Monica places her rounded hands over her eyes like binoculars, "why not Ray, let's sneak a peek."

The spy's stroll in the direction of 1337, the number adorned above the second set of concrete steps leading to Marco's home. Passing the stoop, Marco opens the door, stooping down to tie his shoes.

Monica & Loray say in harmony, "Hiiii."

Smiling, Marco returns 'hi' with a wave.

"I'm Loray and she's Monica, we live down the street and want to to welcome you to the neighborhood."

"Yeah, Jeremy told us you moved in last week," adds Monica.

"Oh, ok; nice to meet you both, I'm Marco. We moved from Chicago; my dad transferred here with his job."

The full view of this brother had both young ladies stuck. The competition flag is gliding up the pole waving for Monica & Loray.

Who will be the one to taste those lips, melt from the embrace of them strong arms, grind on him; gaining the title of Ms. Marco?

He steps down on the sidewalk in front of Monica & Loray, "I'm going for a run around the school track, do yawl run?"

Monica & Loray look at each other with a smirk then look at Marco, "Naaah."

Marco chuckles, "what are yawl doing later?"

Monica blurts out, "nothing, I'm not doing anything; what time will you be back?"

Marco looks on his wrist at his watch, "probably an hour, maybe hour and a half."

Loray grins at Monica, "damn Monie; you sound anxious."

Monica leans closer to Marco, "do you have a pen, I'll give you, my number; call me when you get back, and we can come down."

Waiting for Marco to return with a pen and paper, Loray taps her foot, "wow, you ain't wasting time are ya'."

"Girl, what are you talking bout', I said *we* didn't I?"

Loray shook her head walking off, leaving Marco and Monica to talk.

Loray is coming out the house with a bag of potato chips. Monica casually steps with a bounce up to Loray's porch.

"I know you not pissed Ray."

"Pissed? No, for what, you always compete. I don't trip anymore, makes you look desperate, not me."

Monica's eyes widen, "well Marco and Jeremy went running. Jeremy came back and Marco asked if he was ready, then they left."

Monica & Loray were too close to oppose one another, their friendship resumes, both retreat inside their homes and wait for a phone call from Marco.

After 7 p.m., Loray calls Monica on the phone, "Monie, you heard from Marco yet?"

Monica looks at her cell phone, "no he hasn't called yet, you wanna' walk down to see if he's home?"

"Sure, what you wearin'?" asks Loray.

"Some jeans and a tee shirt, why?"

Loray laughs, "just wondering about your second impression."

"Loray, I haven't given it a second thought; I didn't even realize he hadn't called."

"You lie Monie! you don't have his number to call him, that's all."

Monica sucks her teeth. They hang up and meet on the porch to walk down.

A bush in Jeremy's front patch of yard camouflaged he and Marco, when Monica & Loray arrive in front of the steps.

"Hey guys," says Loray.

Jeremy and Marco look up, "Hey nosy bots," says Jeremy.

Monica squinted her eyes and tightened her lip at Jeremy.

Changing her facial expression while sashaying up the steps speaking to Marco, "we were waiting for you to call, but I see you're busy."

"My apologies ladies, when we got back from running, dinner was ready; moms don't play about dinner time."

Marco and Loray's eyes met at the end of his sentence; Loray picked up the vibe, "Loray, right?" Marco points.

"Yes, that's my name."

"You must be the silent type."

Jeremy chimes, "psht, her? maaaan, don't let that smooth taste fool you, she just as feisty an ornery as the one standing next to her."

Loray sneers at Jeremy, "and you're the same jackass you've always been."

"See what I'm saying man?"

Marco laughs. Loray feels the stare from Monica, and Monica's no longer smiling. Loray isn't in the mood for competing.

"Well, ya'll have fun I'm going in the house."

Marco stands up to stop her, "Loray, why you leaving?"

"I have some reading to catch up on; Monie call me lata'." Loray steps away, walking home.

Marco returns to his stoop, sneaking one more look at Loray, resuming the rest of the evening with Monica and Jeremy, hanging out.

The clock struck twelve; Monica's mother was calling her cell phone, "Hey ma, I'm down the street at Jeremy's-I'm on my way."

Marco escorted Monica home, "I enjoyed hanging out with you Monie, your real cool."

"Thanks Marco, you're cool too."

Monica rubs up against him grabbing his hand, "so can I get your number now, I'm sure you're not the shy type."

Stuttering, he says; "Me? nahhh, umm, well, sure why not."

Monica drops his hand, "You gotta girlfriend or left one in Chicago."

Marco pulls away, "yeah, I think you're super cool Monica, and I would give you, my number; it's just I need to get some things straight before I try something new."

Monica shook her head up and down, "OK, I can understand that I want your undivided attention anyway."

Monica kisses Marco on the cheek, blushing and switching to her front door.

In her bed, Monica recollects the evening kiss, falling asleep hugging her body pillow, imagining her and Marco intertwined.

Saturday morning, Monica woke up and called Loray.

"Hello?"

"Wake up Loray, I need to talk."

"Talk about what girl, its 8:00 on a Saturday morning."

"Marco girl, wake uuuup Loray."

"Uuuuggghhh!" Loray sits up.

Monica explains every topic in detail the three discussed last night and how much fun they had. After an hour, Monica catches a breath.

"Wow Monie, so you think he has some drama in Chicago huh?"

"Yes girl, he said he doesn't wanna start anything new until he took care of that."

"Well, Monie, you know what that means."

"Yeah, another chic still has his heart. Aight; enough about him Ray, what you tryna' do today?"

"After I wake up let's go to the mall, I need a new lip gloss." says Loray.

They hang up.

Getting off the bus, on the way home Loray & Monica see Jeremy and Marco coming from the corner store.

"Hey you two." shouts Loray.

Jeremy and Marco turn around, "hey, what's up?" says Marco, smiling at Loray.

Monica watches Marco's smile at Loray, and grabs his arm, "I saw something in the mall I know you'll like Marco; I didn't get it because I wanted to make sure it was ok first."

Surprised and now uncomfortable, Marco responds, "Wow Monica, that's nice, but you don't have to."

Kissing Marco on the cheek, "I know, but I want to."

"Ewwwwww,' screeches Jeremy, 'you are hot girl."

Loray senses attitude in Jeremy and Monica with Marco.

Loray didn't want any part of the triangle, so she played the square. "Hey, I'll catch ya'll later."

Marco reaches for Loray's arm, "Loray, why won't you hang out with us for a minute?"

Monica pulls away from Marco, with her hands on her hips.

"Naah, I'm tired from walking the mall; plus, I'm hungry and my mom is like yours when it comes to dinner."

Loray walks off smiling, understanding what's really happening. If she plays the cards right, she will hit Blackjack.

After dinner, Loray retired to her room, closing the evening out with confidence, she is ahead of the game Marco is playing.

Nine p.m., Loray receives a call from Monica, "OK, so what's going on with you avoiding everyone Ray?"

"Monie, I'm not in competition with you for Marco, that's all.' 'That's why I leave, so you can have time with him.' But lemme' ask you this, have you thought maybe he doesn't like aggressive females?"

Monica gets an a-ha, moment, "I am all over him every chance I get."

"Yeah,' declares Loray, 'so why do I want to compete with that."

"I think he's still trippin' over Chicago, whoever she is.' 'He must've been in love fa realll." says Monica.

"Monie, why don't you let Marco sit back and *breeeathe* for a few days."

"You're right Loray."

Monica & Loray exchange a few more topics of discussion, hanging up at midnight.

Sunday morning, Loray is awakened from the smell of fresh brewed coffee. Her mother is getting ready for church and yells up to her.

"Loray, I'm leaving for church, will you go in the basement and put the clothes in the dryer for me; then set the trash out for pick up tomorrow."

From the top of the staircase Loray manages to drag out her throat: "Ok mom."

Around noon, Loray jumps up from sleep remembering what her mother asked of her. Running to the basement opening the dryer, clothes still cling to the sides, partially dry. Loray pushes the rinse & spin cycle again.

Returning upstairs, she checks and changes all the upstairs trash cans. With bags in tow coming downstairs the click of the spin cycle alerts her.

Stuffing the smaller bags in the bigger bag, she opens the back door. After tying the larger bag, Loray pushed the garage door open.

Dragging the bag to the plastic bin marked 'trash', Loray looks to the left in the alley, then to right observing two bodies at the bottom of Jeremy's back steps.

She was about to walk down, stopping at the end of the garage, witnessing some strange behavior. Then they kissed.

"Oh my God,' Loray said silently covering her mouth, 'Marco is gay, but Jeremy?"

Loray kept quiet, trying to process the scene and swallow it, but she had to tell Monica. They have been friends too long; Loray didn't want Monica playing herself any longer.

One o'clock and Monica's name glows on Loray's phone.

"Hey Loray, you up?"

"Yeah, I been up; you know mom's go to church on Sunday. She asked me to do some chores."

"Loray, giirrrrl I been thinkin' bout Marco all morning, he is probably a good kisser."

Loray snickers, "Yeah, I bet he does, but you may never find out."

"Don't say that Loray, he just needs some time like you said, so I'ma' lean wit' it, rock wit' it and chill a few days."

Sighing, Loray can't hold it, "Monie; you may have to lean back period. He's not into you."

"Whateva' Loray; or does he like you now?"

"Nooooo, I don't think he likes me either. Let him get over whateva' little problem he left in Chicago. Chill Monie, let him come around, trust me; you will be glad you did."

"Loray, once again you're right. I'd rather wait so I can have him with no interruptions. So, whats on the agenda today?' Are we doing hair and nails today or what?"

"That sounds like a plan Monie, I need some nail polish remover first tho'."

"Well put some clothes on and let's go," says Monica.

They leave for the beauty supply store, which is in the direction of Jeremy's and Marco's. Loray can't look up at the porch after viewing Jeremy and Marco kissing.

Monica looks and smiles, "I wonder what he's doing now."

Loray remains silent. On the way back on the block, Jeremy is walking up Marco's steps.

"Hey you two, what's up?"

Loray & Monica speak, "heeey."

Monica stops to talk to Jeremy, inquiring about Marco to see if he's awake.

"That's why I'm coming to his house, we're going to play basketball."

An excited Monica claps her hands, "Ohhhh, I get to see those legs."

Jeremy looks at Loray-whose head is facing the ground- and Monica.

Jeremy gets in Monica's face with conviction, "why are you such a hot ass Monica?"

Loray looks up at Jeremy wanting to scream about what she saw, but like a lioness, she lays low, waiting to attack.

Monica blocks her face, gesturing like Jeremy's breath stinks, "Damn Jeremy, why so brutal?"

Jeremy lays it out, "because Monica; it's obvious the past three days you been trying to get next to him and he keeps brushing you off."

Loray adds fuel, "Dang Jeremy, you're taking this waaaay too personal, any other time it doesn't matter what Monie and I do."

Jeremy catches himself, "I'm just saying, she's throwing herself on that man, and he ain't biting."

Loray creeps another taunt in, "like I said Jeremy, this one you are taking too far."

Monica steps back discerning the seriousness in Loray's face.

"What's wrong Loray?"

Loray, still focused on Jeremy, firmly asks: "whats wrong Jeremy?"

Jeremy sits on the steps, "what do you mean Loray?'

"Why are you acting defensive?"

Stepping closer to Jeremy, "I find it strange how all these years on the block, you tried every female and when you couldn't get none, started hanging around us.

'Now Marco moves in, and you are concerned with how *he* reacts. Are you doing this to protect us, or do you like Marco?"

Shocked, Monica is confused, "Loray, WHAT IS YOUR PROBLEM?"

Jeremy turns away.

Loray bends down to Jeremy's face, "No Jeremy; answer the question, what's really going on with you and Marco?"

Marco comes outside, "Hey ya'll what's up?"

Once again, Loray walks off with Monica following behind her.

"Loray! Loray! why you go off on Jeremy like that girl?"

Marco and Jeremy approach them.

Marco asks, "Loray, what's going on with you and Jeremy?"

Loray whips around, "Marco, the question should be, what's up with *you* and Jeremy?"

Marco looks down at the ground sighing, Jeremy runs in the house. Monica is standing in amazement, awaiting an answer.

"So, I guess you picked up on it, huh?" says Marco.

"Not at first, but I watched how Jeremy reacts to you when Monica is around, and how you really try to hold it together. This morning I received confirmation when I saw you two kissing out back."

Monica kneels on the ground, "Hell naaah!! You mean to tell me I've been playing myself."

Loray kneels by Monica, "I wasn't completely sure until this morning."

Marco apologized to them, asking Loray & Monica not to disclose anything. Monica was furious but promised to keep it on the hush.

Marco knocked on Jeremy's door and went in to calm and smooth things over. Loray & Monica sat on Loray's porch in shock. Happy the facade was over.

The four teens remained good friends and neighbors. Jeremy & Marco have managed to keep their relationship quiet for the moment, planning a coming out party after graduation. Monica has learned to be patient with relationships and Loray wants to write mysteries.

Superphysi(c)ial Adicktion-11/13/2010 (revised 2022)

Awakened by roaring snores from hard, passionate sex. Red numbers from the clock on his nightstand read: 1:30 a.m. The night light plugged in the wall by his bedroom door, exposes shadows of disarray when we're locked in it—speaking of—"how did that get up there?"

You know the sex is good when you fall into a-coma-like sleep.

But why am I here? Why do I continuously attach myself like a bedbug between his sheets?

Entangled in his smile, his physique—the appendage dangling from his lower torso. This is the shenanigan that keeps me running back. After *'five hours';* the energy is gone.

I'm adickted to his physical appearance.

His arrogant mind or intellect is like a bag of rocks. His body is the 'Arc of the covenant' we have—to be worshiped; idolized.

We practice this 'safeguarded' ritual-strapped up-religiously three nights a week. The other four nights are probably reserved for the rest of his harem.

Should I feel special? Should I feel like he cares for me more than the others? I came to realize my daddy issues when I turned 28.

To experience a non-cheating; unselfish, egoistic male role model leading a household is rare. Women in my family settled. Submitted for security to have a home, title of *'wife'* and money.

I will commit to that when a 'man' shows he's worth it.

I'll remain single and celibate. Medically free from yeast infections and bacterial infections, associated with men's unprotected infidelity.

A plethora of wives and girlfriends/side chicks, share the same man. I call yawl, the BV crew. Swapping their vaginal excretions back and forth. Don't you ladies know men are carriers? he's carrying the same 1+infection back and forth.

Remember ladies, some sexually transmitted infections have no symptoms, and you may not be able to conceive when you really want to have a baby, because you've been carrying a STI since you were 15.

His snoring is loud, his disposition sucks, but damn he has the best rhythm in any position. He gets fascinated by my facial expressions when we're stroking each other.

When I moan—he expands-his eyes closing; my sound barrier gives him authority to go faster; my pitch and tone get higher.

He's holding me now, breathing on my neck: he smells like me, I smell like him; ut-oohh, I'm tingling again. Should I turn around and kiss him so he can shut up?

I soooooo want to leave but, the ego in my tingle must be satisfied first. Since we're both opportunists'—If I play with his left nipple, he will surely rise.

"Ummm, what you doin' baby? You must want some more."

"Yes, I do."

He's up now-literally-playing with my breasts; rubbing against me with a bone hard rod. Yeah, time to strap up so I can saddle up.

Here we gooooo……

The bright rays of the sun sneak through vertical blinds. I awaken, he's in the bathroom performing his morning routine. I hear the toilet flush, the water running.

He emerges from the bathroom naked; I sit up.

My head leaning in my hand, "good morning," I say.

Leaning down to kiss my forehead, "good morning sexy ass, how are you feeling this new day?"

"I'm good."

"Yes, you are, my love, " he says.

He deserves an Oscar. I know once I step outside his front door, he'll forget this moment.

I mention to him: "I'm off tomorrow, would you like some dinner?"

Fumble.

See, I'm hip to the game. He forgot which one I was: prompting an argument on Sunday because I inquired about a text he sent.

Flag on the play, too many players on the field plus a false start.

I'm his Halftime entertainment. When I reach the fifty-yard line into his territory; he hit the locker room to confirm his plays for the rest of the week, and the next game.

I'm a cheerleader on his sexual sideline. The one who no longer wants to be on the playing field.

Lemme' explain I'm Tuesday, Thursday and late Sunday night. You would think his ass was married, but he's not.

He plays the piano like Ray Charles; we're the ones blind to his deceit: at least the rest may be. He satisfies my sexual nature. The emotional attachment detached 8 months ago.

    I found out he played me on Sunday because one of his other boo's wanted to show him off at her birthday party. One of my home girls was at the party.

He wasn't caught, per-say; but he was in the background. My home girl was the private 'eye' and told me he was all in her grill at the party.

I haven't said anything to him, just playing my part.

The birthday girl pictures assaulted my conscious, an all-out investigative tactic kept me busy in his business the whole week. A form of confirmation to me, that I really need to move on.

I'm waiting for a new conversation, new smile—you know-new experiences.

I've known him too long to just jump out there, and he is safer to stroke than a one-night stand.

Don't get me wrong, sex isn't all we do. We go out a lot when we're together, but only to places he won't run into whoever else he has tucked in his pocket.

I know condoms break, but he knows how far to take it with me too; some dudes will try you the first night. If you smell edible and have a clean bathroom and kitchen; they know your coochie clean. They'll try to talk that exclusive, unprotected sex the next time.

Keep you a condom or two in your purse ladies. When he starts, pull out that condom and royally state: "No condom, no cookie." Save your lives sista's.

     Home now, flashbacks of last night keep me content for the next twenty-four hours.

I switched shifts this week and off work on tomorrow (Wednesday).

Taking time to clean my home; scheduled an appointment for a mani & pedi, at 6:00p.m. and

did some grocery/window shopping. Coming from the nail shop, I get a text from him.

"Hey love, won't be able to see you tomorrow, working late."

In my mind, I'm saying: "REALLY?? This is the best you can do??"

I text back: "Since I'm closer to your job, why not spend the night at my place, bring a change of clothes. You have a toothbrush here already?"

Ya'll, know this is a test; right?

He declines, instantly.

Knew what that meant. Must be another birthday blow up from one of the others.

I accepted his 'lie(n), deciding to make plans with my homies. I called my home girl who was at the birthday party first, then called best friend. We made plans for a bowling night.

Tonight, my best friend had to work another shift at the last minute, unable to make it.

Wednesday nights is league bowling, after 9 p.m., more lanes open.

We arrive at 9:30, get our shoes and plan to bowl three games and leave.

The lane to the left of us, was populated with three handsome men, who were checking us out.

To the right was a beautiful young lady sitting alone, we speak.

I was typing our bowling names, when a shadow of a man came from behind.

One of the brotha's to the left spoke while searching for a ball behind us.

I swing around to speak back and guess who I lock eyes with.

Yep, him; I swing forward facing the bowling lane, then swing back because I knooow, I must be dreaming—he is caught and stuck.

He was carrying two pair of shoes, his & hers; there are no more available lanes, and they arrived before we did.

Amazing how wide his eyes got. I played it off and resumed what I came there to do.

My home girl was pissed, I smirked stepping up to bowl.

She laughed and said in a loud pitch, "This son of a bitch is bold."

STRIKE! I turn to walk back; he's sweating bullets and fidgety.

One of the brotha's to the left says: "Damn baby, you come out throwing bows."

I smiled and said, "thank you boo."

My home girl bowls a strike, the brotha's to the left applaud.

My turn: STRIKE! My home girl bowls another strike.

The brotha sitting closest to us was Puerto Rican, umm; and fiiiiine, he breaks the ice with a high five.

"Whats your name?" He asks.

I turn away from him, to get one final look at ole' boy, "Catia, what's yours?"

"Diego," he replies.

Diego was average 5'9 height, dark wavy hair, thin mustache, thick goatee with them damn bushy eyebrows: Ayee Papi! Everyone resumes their games.

My home girl and I were packing up to leave.

The young lady he was with commented on how well we bowled.

Looking in *his* face I respond: "Thank you, sweetie." He turns away.

Diego steps to me, blocking *his* view and asks if we were leaving.

"Well, our plan was to bowl 3 games and go home."

The brotha in my home girls face, wasn't having it, "Don't worry baby, we got ya'll."

He left with his date, I guess to bump and grind, while I played and laughed all night.

Friday, I receive a text: "hope you had fun last night." I don't respond.

An hour later he calls, I don't answer, and he goes straight to voicemail:

"Hey, I apologize; I know I'm caught and you're mad, can we talk about it over dinner tonight?"

His voice fades away as I read the digits of the incoming call on my phone now: "Diego".

I answer the phone, "hey you; how are you?"

New conversation, new smile, you-know, planning new experiences.

      We talked all night like high school sweethearts. Diego works Saturday and I don't wanna be too pushy. We shared personal stories and life history all week, I'm cooking dinner for us Sunday, after dinner will determine if Diego remains late Sunday night, or every Sunday.

ANGEL'O

Leaving her girlfriends down the street in another bar, Tonya sat at the bar in a dimly lit restaurant; alone. She needed to breathe and stop thinking of him: the one she let go of last week, when she caught him in a lip lock with another female.

She is tired. Tired of constant disappointment from men she held close to her heart, but in return held her by a string.

Second sip of her third drink, she felt pressure of a stare to her right.

A subtle glance and she noticed him.

Squinting, to adjust her eyes from the light overshadowing him, she smiled then turned away.

"Lord, not tonight," she said under her breath.

She looked up again in his direction; he's gazing at her still. Pulling her cell phone from her purse checking the time.

12:30 a.m. flashed upon the screen, but she was determined to finish this $7.00 drink.

Sipping again, Tonya maneuvered facing away from him to fake, like she's watching the silent video on TV.

Another sip she feels a presence, knowing he's behind her.

"Hello sweetness," she hears in her ear.

She turns, "hi."

"I know you hear this often, but you are a lovely sight to behold."

Smiling, she thought his interpretation was unique, "thank you."

Now, she could smell the freshness of his cologne, paired with a woman's perfume.

"Is this your first time here?" he asks.

"Yes, it is how did you guess, are *you* a regular?"

"Yes, I am,' he summons the bar tender: 'please give this young lady another of whatever she's drinking."

Tonya puts her hand out, "No, no, please I'm having a hard time finishing this one I have; if it wasn't $7.00 and watered down, I would've left by now."

"Why, the night is young. 'I would like a sample of your conversation, some eye contact, and a smile before I watch you walk away from me."

Tonya lowers her head toward the counter, then looks him in the eye: "here is your eye contact, listen closely to this sample of my conversation:

'This here; is not what I intend for tonight, not being callous, just not in the mood to meet anyone." She politely smiles.

He leans back, "Oh, I get it, you must've broken up with someone recently you cared about."

"You guessed right,"

Extending her arm: 'I'm Roberta Flack, and you are strumming' my pain with your fingers. And you are?"

He laughs, "I'm Donny Hathaway, and you've gotta friend."

'Listen Roberta—"

"Tonya, my apologies, my name is Tonya."

"Listen Tonya, I've seen this kinda hurt before and often enough to know— ".

"To know what,' she interrupts,

'To know that I really don't wanna talk about it anymore.

I'm hurting, pitying and need to hear the right words in a drunken stupor to open my legs wide for a one-night stand?' No thank you sir, I'm good."

He straightens up, "Wow baby, *my* apologies, wasn't expecting all that. I was hoping to make you smile with some small talk, maybe some dinner soon."

Tonya released, "forgive me. It's just, I've been talking about that relationship all week and don't want to keep reliving it, that's all."

He lifts her hand, kissing it, "here's my card, I hope you use it soon; I'm going out of town in a couple of days and really want to see you for dinner before I leave. Would like something beautiful to remember while I'm gone."

He walks away.

Tonya placed the card in her purse.

The last swallow of her drink goes down, she dropped a tip in the jar and walks out the bar.

Sitting in her car; Tonya pauses on the experience she just had and begins crying. Wiping her eyes, she realized she did not read his card, she didn't know his real name.

Fumbling in her purse to retrieve his card, Tonya thought about him kissing her hand: "how old is he, men don't even do that anymore."

She thought about his calm, soothing voice.

Retrieving the card from the bottom of her purse, she read the name: "Angel'O, thank you for entertaining me with your presence, to reach me again, just say my name."

Tonya thought it was a joke, and laughed, "it's all kinda freaks in this world, huh—Angel'O."

Turning the key to start her car, she was startled by a tap on her window.

His smile damn near blinded her.

Tonya advances to roll the window down with no fear.

"Hey, I just read your card."

"And you said my name,' he says.

'So, when would you like to have dinner, we can talk about anything."

Living room intimacy

As I pulled the curtains back, you pulled in the driveway. A smile and excitement took over my body awaiting your kiss and hug greeting. You entered our home, looked over to me smiling.

"Hi baby."

Instantly my nipples salute you like a soldier, waiting for the commander to walk by.

Laughing and moaning, you pinched one and nibbled on the other, "ummm."

Picking me up, my legs automatically swing around your hips, heels touching your ass, yeah, I felt that.

You angled to lay me on the couch, "Umm umm, I feel like a rider today, an equestrian."

You sit, legs apart, I watch you rise like the fresh bread in the oven, then we kiss.

No lights, except the stove and your rock is cooking now.

I whisper: "You miss me today boo?"

Your silence of concentration shows you are: Ready. Set. Pow! Our living room was the Preakness. I mounted, you slouched. I adjusted, you bolted. Slowly I bounce.

Before you laid your head back a slap on my ass says: faster pace, bouncing harder your sweat dripping. Deeper thrusts perched my ass higher.

Thirty minutes later we passed the finish line. The rabbit was tired and so were we. Four legs quivering, sweaty mane and tail. Unwrapping my arms from around your neck like reigns, you say:

"Ride em' girl."

Untangling from you, palms connect another smack of the booty. Washing my hands: "You ready to eat husband."

Licking your lips with that naughty grin you say: "let me know when *you* ready."

Grabbing a plate from the cabinet, to serve you, we eat. You ask: "Did you fix desert baby? 'Never mind just get the bowl of fruit and we can be creative."

Pineapple rings for me, fruit custard for him. Chow!

NEW FACE VALUE

POEM: **New 'Face' value**

Face value: The superficial appearance or implication of something, (Google)

The eyes-say poet/ prophets of conspiracy theories/ broken hearts/ lifelong dreamers, whose eyes burn red passionately/ for 'mass appreciation' from what people don't see in the bat's eyes-blindness.

Poets are the walking parables of prophets from Abraham to Farrakhan/ they shout from platforms of wilderness/ planes, buses, trains & cars/ play music in the ears to drown out the truth/ people want to hear a beat/ not words preached & why poets can't compete/

so, the world remains/ swaying to the (w)rap of the rhythm & blues/ the world can't destroy third eye view.

Gray is the 'mental' state of me/ Environ-metal slabs & concrete/ genocidal chemicals we all breathe=allergies/

The ribbon symbolizes the inhalation/ the new version I be/ stress from the 'mass' of society/ seizure of growth was stunting, and my gift to be free-was running/ out/

no podium plea/ I was on stage 3-biopsy/ so close to my speech/ the Most High intervened/ "You need to speak".

The mouth stretches wide saying: STRENGTH/ bones prostrate in submission/ face value down in humility/ limbs about face from weights pressing on sanity/

when I woke up in the back of an ambulance-another chance/ to happen-stance/ praise is due to the Most High God/for the smile in my spirit/ the gift in the present & the Abraham method.

created May 2018

www.ingramcontent.com/pod-product-compliance
Lightning Source LLC
Chambersburg PA
CBHW032059150426
43194CB00006B/582